YOU KNOW YOU ARE

A TEACHER...

by Richard McChesney

illustrated by Woolly

You Know You Are A Teacher... takes a humorous look at life as a teacher, both inside and outside of the classroom. With 40 illustrated captions, the reader will be laughing in no time.

This is the seventh book in the popular "You Know You Are" series, and has been compiled based on contributions from teachers, their students, family and friends.

Other books in the "You Know You Are" series are:

- You Know You Are A Runner...
- You Know You Are A Nurse...
- You Know You Are An Engineer...
- You Know You Are A Dog Lover...
- You Know You Are A Golfer...
- You Know You Are Getting Older...
- You Know You Are A Mother...

Visit www.YouKnowYouAreBooks.com to join our mailing list and be notified when future titles are released, or find us at www.facebook.com/YouKnowYouAreBooks, or follow us on twitter (@YouKnowYouAreBK

You Know You Are An Teacher...

STRICTLY
BUSINESS

YOU KNOW YOU ARE A TEACHER WHEN YOU FIND YOURSELF SAYING "GOOD JOB" TO YOUR SPOUSE FOR DOING THE DISHES...

YOU KNOW YOU ARE A TEACHER WHEN YOU HAVE GONE TO THE GROCERY STORE UNKNOWINGLY WEARING AN EMBARRASSING STICKER ON YOUR BACK...

I SUCK AT MATH

YOU KNOW YOU ARE A TEACHER
WHEN "BACK TO SCHOOL" SIGNS IN THE
SHOPS MAKE YOU WANT TO CRY...

YOU KNOW YOU ARE A TEACHER
WHEN YOU CAN EAT YOUR LUNCH IN
2 MINUTES, 18 MINUTES SECONDS...

YOU KNOW YOU ARE A TEACHER WHEN YOU BELIEVE THE TEACHERS' LOUNGE SHOULD BE EQUIPPED WITH A MARGARITA MACHINE...

Teachers lounge

YOU KNOW YOU ARE A TEACHER WHEN YOU FEEL THE URGE TO TALK TO STRANGE CHILDREN AND CORRECT THEIR BEHAVIOR WHEN YOU ARE OUT IN PUBLIC...

YOU KNOW YOU ARE A TEACHER
WHEN YOU FEEL THE NEED TO TIE
YOUR HUSBAND'S SHOE LACE...

YOU KNOW YOU ARE A TEACHER WHEN YOU DON'T WANT CHILDREN OF YOUR OWN BECAUSE THERE ISN'T A NAME YOU CAN HEAR THAT WOULDN'T ELEVATE YOUR BLOOD PRESSURE...

YOU KNOW YOU ARE A TEACHER
WHEN YOU HAND PIECES OF PAPER TO
YOUR FRIENDS AND MAKE THEM SPIT OUT
THEIR GUM IN FRONT OF YOU...

YOU KNOW YOU ARE A TEACHER
WHEN YOU GET A SECRET THRILL OUT
OF LAMINATING THINGS...

School
Laminating Room

DIVORCE
DECREE ABSOLUTE

YOU KNOW YOU ARE A TEACHER
WHEN YOU ALWAYS HAVE A BOTTLE OF
WINE HANDY WHEN MARKING BOOKS...

YOU KNOW YOU ARE A TEACHER
WHEN YOU FEEL THE URGE TO TELL
KIDS OFF WHEN OUT SHOPPING...

YOU KNOW YOU ARE A TEACHER
WHEN YOU HAVE THE MOST OUT
OF DATE SPORTS GEAR...

YOU KNOW YOU ARE A TEACHER WHEN YOU HAVE OBSERVED HOW THE VENTILATION SYSTEM IN YOUR CLASSROOM AFFECTS THE FLIGHT PATH OF PAPER AIRPLANES...

YOU KNOW YOU ARE A TEACHER
WHEN MEETNG A CHILD'S PARENTS
INSTANTLY ANSWERS THE QUESTION,
"WHY IS THIS KID LIKE THIS"...

YOU KNOW YOU ARE A TEACHER

WHEN YOU PICK UP LITTER EVEN WHEN
YOU AREN'T AT SCHOOL...

YOU KNOW YOU ARE A TEACHER
WHEN YOU THINK PEOPLE SHOULD BE
REQUIRED TO GET A GOVERNMENT PERMIT
BEFORE BEING ALLOWED TO REPRODUCE...

YOU KNOW YOU ARE A TEACHER
WHEN YOU TAKE IT UPON YOURSELF
TO TRY OUT NEW TEACHING
METHODS ON STUDENTS...

SCHOOL
INFORMATION
TRANSFER CENTRE

YOU KNOW YOU ARE A TEACHER
WHEN YOU START SAVING OTHER PEOPLE'S
TRASH BECAUSE YOU CAN USE THAT TOILET
PAPER TUBE OR PLASTIC BUTTER TUB FOR
SOMETHING IN THE CLASSROOM...

YOU KNOW YOU ARE A TEACHER
WHEN YOU SEND ANOTHER ADULT
TO DETENTION FOR USING FOUR
LETTER WORDS IN PUBLIC...

YOU KNOW YOU ARE A TEACHER
WHEN YOU WOULD RATHER RECEIVE
A BOUQUET OF FRESHLY SHARPENED
PENCILS OVER ROSES!...

Teacher of the Year Award

YOU KNOW YOU ARE A TEACHER
WHEN YOU'VE TRAINED YOURSELF TO GO TO
THE TOILET AT TWO DISTINCT TIMES OF THE
DAY, LUNCH AND BREAK TIME...

toilet

Throne

JOHN

GENTLEMEN

Loo

CLOAK
ROOM

CAN

JERRY

Lavvy

Khazi

Wash
Room

The Dunny

Latrine

YOU KNOW YOU ARE A TEACHER
WHEN YOUR TEAM GOES OUT TO DINNER TO
CELEBRATE THE NEWS THAT YOUR BIGGEST
HEADACHE IS MOVING TO ANOTHER DISTRICT...

YOU KNOW YOU ARE A TEACHER
WHEN YOUR PERSONAL LIFE COMES TO A
SCREECHING HALT AT REPORT CARD TIME...

YOU KNOW YOU ARE A TEACHER
WHEN YOUR ARMS HAVE STRETCHED
BECAUSE OF ALL THE BOOKS YOU
HAVE TO BRING HOME...

YOU KNOW YOU ARE A TEACHER
WHEN YOU WANT TO SLAP THE NEXT PERSON
WHO SAYS "MUST BE NICE TO WORK 9 TO 3
AND HAVE SUMMERS OFF"...

So... are you a
Teacher?

You have just read the seventh book in the popular "You Know You Are" series.

Other "You Know You Are" books are:

- You Know You Are A Runner...
- You Know You Are A Nurse...
- You Know You Are An Engineer...
- You Know You Are A Dog Lover...
- You Know You Are A Golfer...
- You Know You Are Getting Older...
- You Know You Are A Mother...

If you enjoyed this book why not join our mailing list to be notified when future titles are released – visit www.YouKnowYouAreBooks.com, or find us on facebook (www.facebook.com/YouKnowYouAreBooks), or follow us on twitter (@YouKnowYouAreBK)

Other 'You Know You Are' books include:

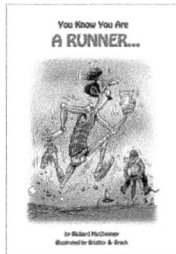

You Know You Are
A RUNNER...

You Know You Are
A NURSE...

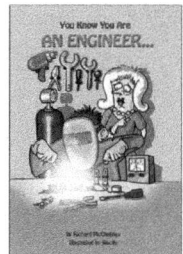

You Know You Are
AN ENGINEER...

You Know You Are
A DOG LOVER...

You Know You Are
A GOLFER...

You Know You Are
GETTING OLDER...

You Know You Are
A TEACHER...
Teacher of the Year Award

You Know You Are
A MOTHER...

Visit www.YouKnowYouAreBooks.com for further details.

www.ingramcontent.com/pod-product-compliance
Lightning Source LLC
Chambersburg PA
CBHW071626040426
42452CB00009B/1509